The Long Stone

and Other Treasures

The Long Stone and Other Treasures

© Copyright 2014

Published by Wicklow Writers, Wicklow, Ireland

www.wicklowwriters.blogspot.com

ISBN-13: 978-1500288952
ISBN: 1500288950

The Long Stone and other Treasures

An Anthology of
Wicklow Writers' 2013-14 Season

Table of Contents

Forward

Creative writing groups are notorious for starting with an enthusiastic shout and ending, a few years later, with a whimper. Not so the Wicklow Writers who began in Wicklow Town in 2001, following a creative writing course run by Pam Beacom.

This was a time when self-publishing was still a dirty word and the ebook a figment of our imagination. As one of the founder members of the Wicklow Writers, I'm pleased to say that this did not hinder the intrepid explorers of the written word and, in their initial year, they published their first anthology. Now, several books and a CD later, Wicklow Writers have once again demonstrated their creativity with this impressive e-anthology. In Nora Fleming's insightful words in her poem 'The Path' they are 'making landmarks on the way'.

Like any worthy collection, the poems and prose selected for this ebook inherently belong together. The perceptive and comical writings allow us a glimpse into the minds and hearts of the creators and, as Eithne Wright succinctly says in 'A Tribute to Poets,' into the 'pictures of their own internal thoughts'.

Indeed, the words in this collection reveal pictures of universal truths of love and loss. Although every reader's reaction is unique, when the writer's source of inspiration flows from a deep well of emotion it spills over to offer nourishment to all. Martin Swords in 'A Poet, To His Love,' says 'You are the words I put on paper/The beginning and the end of every line': a universal sentiment in original imagery.

The humour in the various plays throughout this book cleverly balances light and dark moments – both essential elements for stability. In Vera Cait Walsh's poignant play, 'Gramma's Fantasy', we are reminded of the canniness and strength that a long life bestows. In Ganesh Ramachandran's TV drama, 'The Roadettes', the easy development of the script leaves us wanting more. This 'need to know' continues in the short story, 'A Letter Came Today' by Carolann Murphy, as we sit on the couch with Helen wondering what next is in store.

This thread of needing-to-know is taken up in Peter Hickey's 'Genesis: What They Do not Want You to Know' and referring to music he says, 'God later found it necessary to add light merely so that we humans would be able to read the notes.' Looking to the stars, J. Ted Voigt in 'Firmamentalist' reminds us that 'we have far too many towers built of stone/ Not nearly enough built of stars.' While the pace of Ruth Moore's 'Autumn Run' keeps us moving forward, it also returns us home to the burning fire: another source of light.

Edward Ryan's fine wit comes through strongly in his poetry, and his optimism is keenly felt in 'A New Day' as he prepares to 'join this great adventure'. Indeed, this great adventure continues for Wicklow Writers. The 'Long Stone and Other Treasures' is evidence of how persistence in honing a craft, the cutting and the polishing, results in a treasure throve. Laughter, hope and insight spill over these pages offering a sparkling basket of gems to carry home with us.

-Carol Boland
    Poet and Poetry Therapy Practitioner

NORA FLEMING
MARTIN SWORDS
PETER HICKEY RUTH
MOORE J. TED VOIGT
E. J. RYAN EITHNE
WRIGHT BELINDA
WALSH VERA CAIT
WALSH HELENE
PETERSEN GANESH
RAMACHANDRAN
CAROLANN MURPHY

Gifted Hands

She sat on the steps of her thatched house
Brushing her shining silver grey hair,
This she claimed was the result of her
Collection of soft rainwater.
An elegant woman of three score and ten.
Self sufficient in every way,
She looked after her stock and farm
Alone and loved a game of cards.
She had a flare for fortune telling.
Her generosity and charity work had no limit.
She sang in the local choir and joined in
A game of marbles at the crossroads.

She was Mother and Father.
She was the hand of the churn.
She was the foot of the spade.
She was the song of her Singer.
She was the pattern in the Arran Sweater.
She was the sweetness of the fruit.
She was the love of her animals.
She was the scent of the ' Sweet Afton'.
She was the rhythm of the last.
She was the envy of the barber.
She was the song of the blackbird.
The woman with 'Gifted Hands'

A Voice Like a Blackbird

I hear a bright voice singing,
High and sweet soft and low,
If I were a blackbird
I'd whistle and sing.
I climb to the third step
Of the stile and listen,
I can hear but cannot see,
I move further to the gap
In the hedge,
The voice gently carries.
I search for a rock to stand on.
In the distance a line of
Washing is hoisted into the air.
A beautiful dark haired woman
Stands admiring her days work
Blowing in the evening breeze.
The echo of her soft sweet voice
Fades away in the valley.
A precious memory,
A wonderful mother,
A voice like a blackbird.

Freedom

I pay the price of a wayward youth,
Days long and hard ,
A year seems like a century,
The constant echo of opening
And closing locks,
One. Two. Three. Four,
The sound gets closer.
Five. Six. Seven.
The heavy chains rattle
On the metal door,
A plank for a bed,
Claustrophobia setting in,
Dreaming the hours
To freedom.

When I was young
Life was special,
Freedom, friends,
Loving and being loved,
Happiness.
I did no wrong,
Yet, for ten years now
I have not been taken
From this confined space.
Through the seasons
Alone and ignored.
No freedom, no friend,
Not even the gloved hand
Of the food.
I am tired of living,
My stiff joints
My aching bones
My sad sight.
No one cares for my
Ten times seven years.
No hope of freedom,
Inhumanity befriended me.

The Long Stone

We met in the Wicklow Hills
Over seven decades now,
A brief moment for you,
A lifetime for me.
Now you are waiting under the
Laurel tree for the next generation
And some day I will be but a memory.

The finest pillar in the nineteenth century,
You stood straight and tall by the garden gate,
Stonemasons referred to you as a beauty,
The best of Wicklow granite.
Decades turned to centuries,
Modernisation slowly creeped in and
Sadly you were replaced by fancy brick.

Now in a sheltered corner, two small
Stones bear your heavy weight,
You were always a landmark
known as the "long stone".
A waiting place in the game of 'hide and seek'
A finishing post in the game of 'chase'
And a warm place to relax as one
Delved into their favourite book.

After all these years you are there
Glittering in your corner like rich diamonds.
The evening sun peeps over the thatch,
Shimmering shadows dance upon you,
You a part of me.
Me a part of you.
Sometime, soon in your terms of time
They will look at you
To remember me.

The Path

My path is a life long journey
And strangely brings a smile,
Walking along its grassy way
Jumping across each style.

Making landmarks on the way,
Conquering twists and bends,
Purpose, destination
Achievement at the end.

Wavering at the crossroads,
Facing obstacles on my way,
Paving a way to the future
While I trod along each day.

Meandering from place to place,
Deciding which path to take,
Hoping for the right one.
Seven decades later
Still hoping.

A Fly

Clustered up in the cavity
Of an old wooden window,
Huddled closely to my comrades
We slept through the long dark winter.
It's early summer,
We awake from the darkness,
Adjusting to the light,
I bid my friends goodbye.
I am alone.
The hot rays of the sun
Beam from the clear blue sky,
I move freely through the air.
As I bask on the heat of human flesh,
A dark shadow settles above me.
Slams down upon a bare thigh,
Swiftly I manage to escape.
I love the warmth of human flesh,
I dare to try again,
Blissfully dreaming
I rest for a while,
A shadow hovers over me,
But I escape once more.

Moments

Petite figure standing erect
Feet slightly apart
A little shake of the arms
Poised, looking into the unknown
Raised hands
Fingers slowly placed on black and white notes
Introduction.

Eyebrows raised
A gentle smile
A sweet voice fills the church.
Colourful variance of tone
Complements the stained glass windows.
Each exotic language
Transports the mind
And the spirit
Magical
Mystical
Silence
Reaching every note smoothly and sweetly
Soothes the emotion.

Diaphragm open
Long lasting deep breath
Finale.

The Meadow Bank

Taking a deep breath before
Ascending your steep brow
I view the landscape that
Looks down to the Irish Sea.
Memories of my sisters and
Brothers all playing together
In your long grass.
Workmen windrowing hay.
Our grey mare galloping into
The shade from the sun's hot rays.
You brought such variety of
Colour with each season.
Spring, brought sparkling dew
Upon your soft green grass.
Lambs frolicked about
In the morning sunshine.
Summer, brought the sweet
Scent of new mown hay.
Autumn, brought fresh mushrooms.
Winter, mounds of snow lay
Deep upon your high brow.
Hours of joy were spent sleighing
On your steep slope.
In this modern advanced world
Times have changed, the way of
Life has changed and the seasons
Have changed.
The cycles of life continue
But you remain constant.

Through the Underpass

A herd of friesians amble
Homeward along the cow path
From light to darkness and
Into the light again
Home to the promise of relief.
Sometimes our own light dims
We struggle through darkness
And back into the light
Gladdened to be in the light again.

NORA FLEMING
MARTIN SWORDS
PETER HICKEY RUTH
MOORE J. TED VOIGT
E. J. RYAN EITHNE
WRIGHT BELINDA
WALSH VERA CAIT
WALSH HELENE
PETERSEN GANESH
RAMACHANDRAN
CAROLANN MURPHY

When Albert got to t' Pearly Gate

No doubt you'll 'ave heard about
Albert Ramsbottom
And all his adventures to date
But I'll bet you've not heard of what 'appened
When Albert got to t' Pearly Gate.
It was one of those days that was slow, like
And no one was there, 'e could see
'Well that's a fine thing', pondered Albert
Where is t' Gatekeeper with key?'
Now Albert, was no longer 'young' Ramsbottom
Being ninety one years and a week,
'e considered this neglect of duty
And no less than a bit of a cheek.
So taking stick with 'orses 'ead 'andle
'e rapped on t' Gate gold and pearly
Till someone, 'e thought must be Peter, came,
And says, "eh lad but you're a mite early."
"It's not that I'm early", says Albert
"But more likely that you're running late
And I think it's unfair to suggest it
After making an old man stand and wait."
With this t' Gatekeeper felt chastened
So taking key from its hook
'e opened up Gate for our Albert
Saying, "come in lad, I'll look in t' book.
I'm sorry about t' situation
'e said as 'e entered a stall
But we wasn't expecting an intake
This being t' Sabbath an all".
Now Albert being somewhat outspoken
As well as a sceptic to boot
Says, "d' you mean to tell me Gatekeeper
That in 'eaven on Sundays you're shoot"?
"There are some exceptions", says Gatekeeper,
"Such as Royalty and 'eads of t' State
But for ordinary folk there is Limbo
An' there until Monday they wait.

So tell me your name if you'd care to
And I'll check in t' book of t' dead
An' see why you're here on a Sunday
In preference to Monday instead".
"My name is Albert Ramsbottom
From Lancashire, England of late
And I think it a sin to be treated
Like a second class citizen mate".
"Look 'ere my good man", says Gatekeeper,
I'm an ordinary soul, I'm no saint
So I'll send for t' shift supervisor
And to him you can make your complaint".
So t' shift supervisor was sent for
An' when 'e arrived at t' stall
'e says, "'ere what's th' to do then
And this being t' Sabbath an' all"?
The Gatekeeper 'e started explaining
And Albert, 'e tried to speak too,
When t' Super, losing 'is patience
Shouted, "It's like being at ruddy zoo".
So raising 'is 'and for decorum
'e called for Gatekeeper's report.
Then speaking directly to Albert
Says, "You'll get your chance to retort".
Our Albert 'e didn't feel 'appy
About treatment 'e'd got in this place
But 'e managed to somehow keep silent,
Albeit with glare on 'is face.
Gatekeeper 'e told Supervisor,
"There's no record of 'im in t' buke
But you don't need to take my word for it
You're welcome to take a good luke".
"There's no need for that", says the Super,
"your word is as good as can be
But just for the sake of t' complainant
It's better I have a look see.
You're not in t' book Mr Ramsbottom
I cannot explain, but you're not,
It could be a plain simple error
Or simply that you've been forgot".
"Well that's a fine thing", says bold Albert

"Not something that one would expect
That in Heaven one can be forgotten
It's nought but downright neglect".
The Super 'e just wasn't used to
Such language from ordinary sowls
So 'e threatened to expel our Albert
With t' toe of 'is boot in 'is bowels.
One insult begged for another
Till Super 'e finally flipped
'is halo slipped off in t' tussle
And fell on t' floor and got chipped.
Then Albert, 'e says to the Super,
That 'e knew for a fact and could tell
'e wouldn't be subject to treatment
Like that if 'e went down to Hell.
Says Super, "then why don't y' go there"?
An' join up with Lucifer's crew"
"I would if I could says our Albert
But t' was them 'as sent me to you".

A New Day

Dawn dissects my room
dulls the embers
of my night's dreaming.

The street snarls
through the window,
stalks my thoughts.

Stars in hiding,
bird's song
gives praise
to a new day.

I prepare
to join this great adventure.

Coloured Days

Spring crawls out
of winter grey
the green turtle
out of the sea.

Golden summer,
sleeping,
dreams of
gambolling young things
and future wings
taking her swiftly
to the blush of
Autumn plenty.

I mourn
for the passing
of all the coloured days.

Roadside Carcass

I hate to see a dead thing by the way;
life serves no purpose by its waste,
that did not die for purpose sake
but in the cause of human haste.

Haikus

1.   Tried to ride a horse
of course the horse reared, so I
rode the ambulance

2.   Took her by the hand,
my hand touched her breast, that's why
my eye was blackened.

3.   Climbing to great heights
I seen the world around me,
but lost sight of you.

4.   On a winding path
I left no trail to follow,
please find me again.

5.   Why is it funny,
that when I can hear laughter
I too want to laugh.

6.   A season of snow,
too much white for my liking,
I prefer colour.

7.   The wind sighs and blows
for all its puff and bluster
only cleans the air.

8.   Hardest is the rock
persistent is the water
time makes the rock yield.

Monochrome

The merry din of Summer fades away,
Autumn's gaudy colours all but passed,
The fruit trees have given all they may,
Monochrome winter comes like a blast.

The grass is crisp with morning frost,
Ice forms on the garden pond,
I long for the seasons that are lost;
Youthful love and friendships bond.

This season's days are short and drear,
Time, a pitiless, ravenous beast,
Banquets upon each day, each year,
Life's regurgitated feast.

Come Spring, the world new born ,
Brings joy in that rejuvenated dawn.

Popped

The cork was popped with a fizzy pop
And a jolly good draught was taken
Taken well was a jolly good draught
And many a draught was taken
Right to the very lees it was quaffed
Then even the lees were taken
To the very last and jolly drop.

A Funny Thing

A funny thing happened to me the other day on my early morning walk. Well not actually to me but rather in my presence. I met with a certain priest, who shall remain nameless, as I often do, and time allowing, we will spend a few minutes discussing some topical subject of the day, with the exception of religion. The good Father knows that I am an atheist and being a man of exceptional manners and supreme gentleness never brings up the subject. Not that such a conversation would bother me but, and this is only my assumption, it might for some reason, be uncomfortable for him.

On this occasion an over-flying bird deposited its load unto the good Father's hat which turned it from black to black and white. A seagull was my main suspect judging by the volume and colour.

"That's supposed to be for luck," I said, as the good Father removed his hat. At the same time he took a step backwards looking to the sky in an attempt to identify the avian bomber placing his foot, as he did so, in a fresh pile of dog shit that neither of us had previously observed. He proceeded to do, what I can only describe as, the shit-kicker's waltz, in an effort to dislodge the offensive substance, leaving, as he danced, partial footprints in dog shit over a wide area of pavement. During this performance he uttered the most blasphemous words that ever I heard pass the lips of this good and holy man.

"God bllll..ess us," he said, keeping his gaze directed to the heavens, "but isn't it a blessing that dogs don't fly"?

 For my part I could only agree with the good Father and hastily depart before the volcano of laughter inside of me erupted.

The Cat That Walked Backwards

There was a cat that was newly arrived in heaven, cat heaven that is. When she arrived she was interviewed by the admissions cat whose job it was to ask a series of questions.

'Please sit down', he said to the new cat, 'I have a series of questions to ask you'.

'What about'? Asked the new cat, in a somewhat indignant manner. Well she was just not used to being questioned.

'O! This and that, nothing serious really', said the admissions cat, 'it's just for our records you know'.

The new cat, now worried that she might be kicked out of heaven, quickly apologised;

'I....I'm so sorry', she said, 'please go ahead, I'll answer any question that you care to ask'.

'No need to be sorry', said the admissions cat with a kindly purr, 'just answer my questions honestly. So let us begin: How did you meet your end'?

'A dog bit me, it was very painful, it shook me like a rat and tossed my body aside like a piece of rubbish, it didn't even eat me'.

'You let a dog get close enough to bite you', said the admissions cat incredulously.

'I'm sorry', said the new cat, 'but it was not entirely my fault.'

'Don't be sorry', said the admissions cat once more, 'just explain'.

'Well'.....she hesitated a bit...'you see....at the time....I had a can on my head'.

That made the admissions cat sit up and take notice.

'What on earth made you put a can on your head'? He asked.

'I'm sorry but that is not exactly what I meant'.

'DON'T BE SORRY', said the admissions cat, raising his voice for the first time, 'just, please, say what you mean'.

'I did not put the can on my head but rather put my head in the can'.

The admissions cat's eyes began to roll.

'At the risk of repeating myself', he said, 'what on earth made you put your head in the can'?

'There was an enticing smell from within which I simply had to investigate and so I slipped my head into the can where I discovered some tasty morsels of food but when I tried to withdraw my head it would not come out. I walked backwards for what seemed ages but my head just would not come out. I heard the dog coming but could do nothing for I could not see. At first I thought it might help me since the can had contained dog food, but alas that was not the case and so here I am. I'm really sorry for being such a nuisance'.

'You're not being a nuisance and stop apologising all the time it will not help you now. Did you not think to push the can off your head with your paw'?

'No, I didn't think of that because I've always been able to walk backwards out of trouble, this is the first time I've failed'.

'And your last', said the admissions cat, now with a tone of sympathy for the new cat, 'but it was rather stupid of you to do such a foolish thing'.

'Yes, I admit it was a stupid thing to do and my only consolation is the knowledge that somewhere down in the world there is a human being more stupid than me'.

'How did you work that out'? asked the admissions cat.

'Well', said the new cat, 'I only have instincts to guide me. That's why I stuck my head in the can. They are supposed to have the big brains and something called intelligence. If only that stupid human had rinsed out the can before they disposed of it they would have prevented my painful and untimely death'.

'If you were to meet that human and explain all this, what would you expect them to say to you'? asked the admissions cat. The new cat purred for a moment wondering if she should say it. Then she replied, 'they would probably say'...and here she hesitated once more '...I'm sorry'.

NORA FLEMING
MARTIN SWORDS
PETER HICKEY RUTH
MOORE J. TED VOIGT
E. J. RYAN EITHNE
WRIGHT BELINDA
WALSH VERA CAIT
WALSH HELENE
PETERSEN GANESH
RAMACHANDRAN
CAROLANN MURPHY

A Poppy Season

She is a Welcome Home
A room full of people.
She is an egg neatly broken
A Roulade sweetly rolled.
She is a lost recipe
She is her mother
At her mother's knee.
She is the Deb with the frizzy hair.
She is first to cry
And first to laugh.
She is the woman from the Meals on Wheels
She is a wet dog in a blanket
A long walk by the water's edge.
She is a silver rosary
A Hail Queen of Heaven.
She is a missal of memorial cards
A future firmly rooted in the past
In Birth, in Life, in Death,
She is unafraid
She is the mother of two sons, and a husband
She is Mam, but never Mummy
She is busy when there is no need
Is tired too often
She is the strong stem
She is a Poppy in a window

A Poet, To His Love

You are my comma, my full stop.
You are my rhythm and my rhyme
You are the words I put on paper
The beginning and the end of every line

Half Past Midnight Grafton Street

Half Past Midnight Grafton Street
Filling time with only
French fries and a coffee
I'm sat with the lost and lonely
Christmas lights and mannequins
Expensive bags with names on
Glamours chat and giggle over skinny drinks
Avoid the old bag lady hanging on
Still sitting with the empty cup
Watching the world ignore her
Cold tea and a warm seat
Out of the cold and frivolous festive cheer
Half Past Midnight Grafton Street
A tired old lady shuffles out
Out on the cold expensive street
She starts her lost and lonely walkabout

Listening at Sally Gap

There is always a wind
one or other of the four winds blowing
moaning with the loneliness of the place
soft ground tough grass and hard sheep.

Ghosts of silent footed rebels tramping to the
safety of their mountain valley holds
before the Military.
The wind still carries their shouts

Their cries their pleadings and their hopes
mixing with the bleak empty sounds of this place
a trickle of water on stone
a gurgle of water on wet black turf

Is that the thin echo of a sleán slicing sods,
or that heavy hollow sound, the turf-cutter's
clunkin' bottle of sweet milky tea
corked with a scrunch of newspaper

Or a bit of broken fence banging in the wind

Loneliness
After Billy Collins

At edge of town I once saw Loneliness
sitting with his friend Together
sleeping in a shelter.

I, heading home from nightshift to family,
was alone, not lonely.

But they were there together, huddled
for heat in the long cold night.
Each was all they had.

Soon, on some cold or stormy morning
one would fail to wake.
Then the loneliness would double,
being alone, utterly.

Bob Dylan and me.

I know Bob Dylan well.
Grew up with him,
We all did.
He was the voice
We didn't have.
Said the words
We didn't know to say.
Such words.
He saw and sang
Of things we saw
Yet wouldn't speak about.
Where we were awkward,
He was talkin' out.

For forty years
I've looked up,
Listened up, to him.
Now changed, aged, yet
Both forever young,
I'm glad we grew together
In interesting changing times.
We never met,
But it's alright.
We spoke.
We played our parts.
He needed me to listen all along.
The singer sings
So others hear the song.

Keogh Square 1959

Paddy Cardiff and me
selling loose turf around Inchicore.
Me around nine;
he a big lad, maybe twelve.
Pushing the handmade cart
with the metal wheels
like something saved from Warsaw,
into Keogh Square.
The cart felt at home.
Paddy sold a few here and there.
Mind yourself in here he said as
a man approached.
See him said Paddy if he asks for turf for nothin'
give it to him.
And if he asks for the cart, give him that as well

It wasn't easy living
in Keogh Square.
Nor easy making a living
in Keogh Square.

The Birches at Birkenau

'Birkenau' – the Birch Wood.
Gathered among the Beautiful Birches
outside Auschwitz – Birkenau
the Chosen People waited, hoping in vain.
Deliberately deceived, mothers, daughters,
Fathers, sons, frail, infirm, families, waited.
Deceived. Deceived in Life.
Deceived in Death. Delayed only.
The chambers and the ovens full.
No Exodus.
Still waiting, waiting for us.

Lost treasures, among the roots
a button, a gold ring, a child's buckle, survive.
Carved in birchbark a plea – 'remember',
cries out for the lost tribe
this grove once mocked.
The birches and the memory still grow, pointedly,
heavenward, screaming at God.
Golgotha – place of skulls.
Birkenau – place of birches.
Even the trees were corrupted.

Anniversary of Liberation of Auschwitz

The Land of Longing

Welcome to the land
Of the Frothy Frappuccino
Filet Mignon, Lobster Burgers
And Coffee that comes every
Which way but coffee

The best in America seemed
To come from somewhere else
Paris France, London England,
Belgium Belgium, carrying its
Continental Chic to this Big
Brash confident yet
Uncertain country

Only the polished clock
In the local rail station,
The red bonneted
Shiny chromed sixteen wheeler
On the interstate,
And Grand Central
Spoke to me in American.

They said "Howdy".

Newenglanding

White steeples over branches.
White houses made of wood
At home among the trees.
Tall grass and meadows,
Stonewall homes to scampering things.
Sound of cars, grass-cutting people,
Intruding
In quiet calm Connecticut.
New England sunset, sense
Of frogs and Robert Frost.

Split log fence and old walls
Tell tall tales unchanged of
Gentle manners, courtesy and friends.
Peace and order threatened by a new world
Rising, rampant, in an old state.
Yet save the quiet for even' sun,
New England summer evening sitting,
Rocking, Robert Frosting on the porch.
Which road led here?

A Walk In The Woods With Robert Frost

Overcast but warm,
The day dry, unusually.
Walking the woods with the dogs
As many times before.
Lucy and Tiggy, away in the rough dark deepwood,
Yipping with the scent of deer, excited.
Ruby, river scrambling, biting
At the bogwater, wagging her tail,
From the shoulders back

Along the old familiar track, into
The clearing where the roads diverge.
I stopped and stood. Which way to go?
Think of another Poet, and roads not taken.
Yes, I've been here before. This way I came.
That way I saw a squirrel once.
And down that way a badger.
Straight on, the Mill Pond where ducks dabble.
Behind me then a stag, stares my way, and
Startled, slips into the wood.

I think again of Robert Frost and look a different way.
I stand a while. I turn, retrace my steps, recall, relive,
I know, I'll write this down, and this will be
The road I've taken.

Autumnal

Now is the golden browning of the year,
early dusky evenings, and the quiet.
A time of listless leaves and branches,
a settling, and a dignity of dying.

Smells of damp and rolling mist,
now haunt the hedges and the willows
of the river valley field.
The evening bells sound dampened in
the thick of Autumn air.

The year is closing down
to sleep the winter sleep through frost and chill.
Silent snow will follow in its time
sealing the land in white and crispy cold,
freezing in death what life will need to live.

When all is dark in winter, thoughts
of bluebells ringing in the dell
keep hope alive that spring will peal anew.

Phoebe. Like an Angel.

Phoebe hobbled out on bamboo crutches. She looked around and waited. She waited for the effect she knew would come, the hush of quiet anticipation and rapt attention. She paused waiting for the absolute quiet she knew was coming, all conversation stopped, all eyes turned to her as she knew they would. And still she waited, loving every second of the attention. Despite her young years, she managed to focus the room's attention, milking every second, loving every second in the limelight. In a few more seconds, once she was sure they were all paying attention to her and her alone, she would begin.

This was Phoebe's home, the grand drawing room of her home on Stockton Street, just up the hill from Market Square, San Francisco. And this was her special day, her ninth birthday. Born in 1897 on April 17th, she was the favoured youngest child of Mamma and Papa, Mr. Henry Hollings and his beautiful wife Sarah. The Hollings family in their beautiful home were pillars of San Francisco society. Henry was a leader in the community and with Phoebe's two older brothers, James and Edward, together they ran the property empire of Hollings Hollings and Hollings, Real Estate. Phoebe had heard of real estate but didn't know or care what it was. Sometimes when she heard Papa say the words she wondered what was so real about estate, and was there a type of estate that wasn't real. She didn't know or need to know, all she cared about was that she was the apple of Papa's eye, because he kept telling her so.

Now at nearly six p.m. on this her ninth birthday, after playing games with friends and cousins, Phoebe was ready for her party piece in front of all the adults. Much as she liked playing childish party games, being the focus of attention and adulation from the grown-ups, especially Mamma and Papa, was what she craved and planned for.

Three days previously she had sought help from Mai Li, the live-in Chinese housemaid, in preparing for this performance. Mai Li had been housemaid in the Hollings household for over five years now, a full time live-in, part of the family really. She lived in the downstairs one-room apartment off the kitchen with her poor crippled six year old son, Yuen Li. There was no Mr. Li.

Even though Mai Li had been very busy with preparations for Phoebe's party, and minding Yuen Li, Phoebe insisted on asking her for help in planning her party piece. "I want a Chinese wig hat, I want a silk kimono, and I want Yuen Li's bamboo crutches" she insisted, "and I want you to help me with my song," she demanded without saying "please". Mai Li helped even though it meant staying up half the night sewing and stitching, while Phoebe slept, looking forward to her party piece and performance.

She was ready to begin. Yet still she held off. All the room looked at her. At her Chinese style wig. At her silk kimono style costume which Mai Li had made to fit. Even at the beautiful Chinese style slippers which Mai Li had hurriedly made, even though Phoebe hadn't asked for them. And at the bamboo crutches. Phoebe stood and wobbled a bit to emphasise the crutches. She knew full well how to extract every last drop of attention, every last tear on the cheek from the ladies, every last lump in the throat from the men. No one looked anywhere except at her. No one made a sound. She began.

> "Where is my Geisha Lady?
> Where oh where can she be
> She's gone with the Seven Samurai
> To a land beyond the sea"

After this verse there was complete silence, broken only by the faintest sniffle as a tear or two were nearly held back. The plaintiff sound of a two string instrument played by Mai Li started and played on as Phoebe continued

> "Where is my Geisha Lady?
> Why does she not love me?
> Left here to hobble sadly
> A beggar for all to see"

45

She stopped. There was a rapt silence. She bowed. Suddenly
the room erupted with applause, shouts, whistles, and calls of
"Bravo, Bravo". She bowed and bowed and bowed, and
continued to milk the applause, praise, and adulation as all in
the room stood, rushed forward and lifted her on shoulders.
Mamma, Papa, James, Edward, Aunt Lilly and Uncle Teddy
cheered and cried, all at the same time. They loved her. Phoebe
loved it. No time for "Thank You". No time to notice Mai Li
slip away downstairs with her instrument under one arm, and
her son Yuen Li, awkwardly under the other.

Phoebe, shoulder high, waved a bamboo crutch in each hand
as she was waltzed around the room on Papa's shoulders. It
was a great birthday and even though she got lots of presents,
this was the best part.

At eight o'clock it was time for Phoebe to go to bed. Exhausted
and elated at the same time she fought off sleep and sat at the
top of the stairs listening to the grown ups talking and singing
downstairs. Great guffaws of laughter floated upstairs as Papa
told a grown up joke. Mamma and Papa, together, sang "Irene,
Goodnight Irene", and then Edward in his beautiful tenor
voice sang "Just a Song at Twilight". Phoebe loved all these
old familiar songs, especially the sad songs from the old
country like " I'll Take You Home Again Kathleen" , which
everyone now sang together, as always in memory of
Grandmother Kate, the first of the Hollings to settle here. In
between songs she heard her own name mentioned now and
then, and she loved that. "I do declare, that little Phoebe sure
sings like an angel", she heard someone say and she beamed to
herself with pride.

At ten o'clock Mai Li found Phoebe fast asleep with her head
propped against the heavy banister post at the top of the stair.
She lifted her gently and without waking, Phoebe was tucked
into bed in her own little bedroom. Mai Li looked about for
the bamboo crutches but could not find them. She went down
to bed herself in her room off the downstairs kitchen. Yuen Li
was fast asleep in his little cot in the alcove.

By twelve o'clock everyone was gone home and those who were staying in the house were in bed, some talking, some sleeping with the help perhaps of fine wines and whiskies. Soon all would be silent.

Shortly after one o'clock in the morning there was a very slight bump throughout the house, as if a heavy door had banged shut. No one woke and no one noticed. Phoebe turned over in her sleep and continued her dream of being on stage while the audience's applause resounded. In her dream she couldn't leave the stage with her arms full of bouquets, because the audience wouldn't let her go.

Mai Li slept on soundly, hoarding every last wink of sleep before she would rise at her usual time of five thirty a.m., to start the routine of fires, stoves and cooking for the day ahead. She had been extra tired because of the work of helping Phoebe. No one had thanked her for the extra work, not even Phoebe, but then she hadn't been expecting to be thanked, so she didn't sleep in disappointment, only tiredness.

At five o'clock Yuen Li half woke. He didn't know why. He thought of getting out of bed to go to the kitchen for a drink of water. He felt around but couldn't find the bamboo crutches he needed, so he didn't go but stayed in the alcove bed and drifted off to sleep again.

At five twelve the earth moved.

It moved with the sound of forty trains crashing, with the sound of fifty bombs exploding together, with the sound of all last year's thunder rumbling at once.

It moved with a force so great it couldn't be compared to anything, because no one alive had experienced a force so huge and so loud before, and lived to tell about it.

And it didn't stop.

It kept roaring and shaking and ripping and knocking down for over one minute, until virtually everything in San Francisco had been shook and ripped and knocked down and smashed in ruins.

Only Yuen Li woke, alive.

It was ten hours later, though he didn't know it. He was injured but aware. He thought he heard calls and cries but he wasn't sure as he drifted in and out of consciousness. Much later and in a weakened state he was pulled from the protective alcove all that remained of the house, in the wreckage of the once magnificent city. He asked his rescuers, Army and Red Cross personnel, for his mother Mai Li, and Phoebe. They had no answer. No one else woke that night, or any night, in Phoebe's house.

No bamboo crutches were found.

The Holy Hour of Christmas

As usual, Regan came back into the Department office by the back door, so as not to be seen. It was four forty-seven. Seven minutes later than his usual return from lunch. He was raging, red faced and flailing as if he was going to hit someone or something, if he could find something to hit. 'Apoplectic' would have described him but he didn't know that word.

It was the day before Christmas Eve and as a result of his encounter Regan was like a bear with a sore head. He'd had a plan for Christmas, collect the turkey and ham from Haffners and pick up the train for the youngfella', after he'd had a nice few slow pints in Kehoes, and everything would have been grand. But now everything was in a red mist of anger and he couldn't think straight, or at all. "Feck them, feck them all", he muttered loudly to himself and anyone who happened to hear in the hushed and apprehensive atmosphere of the Department of Agriculture office.

Regan had a charmed life and an easy job in the Department, keeping records of live cattle exports for somewhere up the line in the senior section of the Department. No rush, no pressure – keep the numbers flowing more or less on time – and no complaints from the few cattle that were not counted, now long since slaughtered. No complaints either from the cattle numbered in the export figures who had never actually left their farms and were still happily standing in the muck chewing the cud, for the time being at least, while they were being counted twice, to say nothing of being claimed for twice by some right cute farmer. Yes, a handy if somewhat boring job that suited someone like Regan who was fond of a drink, while he took his time slowly and easily getting by as he moved towards his pension all of another fifteen years away. Largely unsupervised, he had his well practiced late lunch routine well honed. It took him often to Kehoes, and as often into the little back snug which could be closed off by Vincent the barman and anyone in it left alone to carry on quietly and unseen well into the Holy Hour with everyone minding their own business.

Regan minded his own business in the snug all right, but he hadn't reckoned on young Garda McCloy from Clones who wanted to mind everyone's business, while looking to make a name for himself up in Dublin.

McCloy had seized his chance to leave the suffocating inactivity of townie Ireland to get down to Dublin and make his mark on the promotion ladder. Unfortunately there were hundreds of other ambitious townie Gardai trying to do the same thing, so McCloy reckoned he'd have to make a big noise and fast if he was to be noticed.

Regan had settled nicely on the high stool beside the hatch inside the snug having had a few outside with the regulars before the Holy Hour. The pub had cleared quickly at Vincent's urging and Regan slipped quietly, as often before, into the darkish back snug just as Vincent locked the front doors of the pub, turned off the lights, and all went quiet. Regan had ordered another pint and a chaser, and a round of thick ham and cheese sandwiches by way of lunch and they all stood settling on the counter for Regan to address, when there was loud knock knock on the closed front door. "Gardai, open this door", boomed a loud voice which Regan could hear way in the back snug. Vincent, flummoxed by this event which had never happened before had no choice but to open the door and in strode Garda McCloy, talking loudly so as to make his presence felt and authority known. "I have reason to believe......" said McCloy loudly, not finishing his sentence, while looking around. The place was empty.

"Is there any persons here drinking on these premises?" boomed McCloy towards Vincent.

Vincent muttered something non committal, making noise but saying nothing. Just then McCloy sniffed like a bloodhound. Tobacco smoke? Looking earnestly towards the dark back of the pub he thought he saw a faint reddish glow in the dark. He listened very carefully and quietly. Breathing ? With two great bog bounding strides he was at the back snug and barged in noisily to confront Regan - a full fresh pint untouched, a delicate small Jameson, a plate of thick sandwiches with a knife on the edge, and the last of a Player's Navy Cut on the side of an ashtray.

"Well now…" said McCloy officiously, "what have we here? Did you buy that drink during the Holy Hour?"

"I did not Guard," said Regan, technically correct in that he had called the drink a minute before the time.

"Did you sell this man drink during the Holy Hour?" McCloy challenged a trembling Vincent.

"I did not Guard" said Vincent who could just about keep his wits, as Regan had not actually paid for anything yet.

"Well now, doesn't that bate Banagher" said McCloy mockingly in a thickish country townish tone, addressing the smart alecs of Dublin Town. "I may be from the country but I know what I'm lookin' at" said McCloy jeeringly.

"A pint and a small one that no one owns, sandwiches that no one wants, a customer who's not a customer and a barman who sold nothin'."

"Isn't that a marvelous thing entirely, miraculous I'd say, could only happen in smart Dublin."

"But I'll have yis both" he bellowed, getting angry at being made a fool of so he thought. And then he took a step too far in his display of cuteness surrounded by Dublin smartness. He picked up the pint and took a giant swallow, he took one of the sandwiches and ate heartily, and he lifted the Jameson and knocked it back.

"Well if no one owns it, no one bought it and no one sold it – it's a shame to let it go to waste."

"Aw God" said Regan plaintively his mouth hanging and his eyes pleadingly looking at his pint being consumed gulp by gulp. "Could we not maybe join you Guard, in a little hospitality like, with a pint or a small one, all together like, for the Christmas that's in it like."

"You may not" said McCloy. "I didn't order this pint, I didn't pay for this pint, and the barman didn't sell me this pint during the Holy Hour so there's no law being broken, by me."

"You on the other hand were found on the premises during Holy Hour – so you're for the high jump, the long drop", he said mockingly looking Regan in the eye, coldly.

"Yes Guard but you're the one who is drinking on the premises during Holy Hour, whereas I was just looking at a pint."

For the briefest of moments there was a look of winning satisfaction on Regan's face.

For the briefest of moments there was a hint of a smile on Vincent's face.

And for the briefest of moments there was a hint of paused doubt on McCloy's face.

"Look here Regan" said McCloy angrily using Regan's name for the first time indicating that he knew who he was talking to – "you get yourself back to the Department of Agriculture me boyo – I've been watching you for a while and you're for the book – a summons on your desk will soon take the cuteness out of you when the Higher Officers and Assistant Secretaries get to hear of it."

Regan stormed out knowing he was cornered, and 'apoplectic' he was like a bull back in the Dept. office.

"Feck them, Feck them all" he thought – "the Seniors, the Higher Officers, the Secretaries and every cute whore of a Guard that ever came out of the bog and down to Dublin. Feck them!"

It would take Regan a long time to get over this. There would be no Turkey, no Ham and no Train. There would be no

Christmas and probably no New Year. There would be no warmth in the bed, for a long time. And there would be no promotion prospects, not that he wanted any having no gra for responsibility, nor no pension add-ons that might have been taken for granted, not after a summons served in January, and Regan in court in February, and carpeted on the top floor in March for his lax and wayward ways, and the serious failing of getting caught.

And cruelly and ironically there would be no satisfaction for Regan in the final twist in the story. He was too busy sulking and feeling sorry for himself to hear the end chapter. For Regan was not the only Civil Servant, higher or lower, from many Departments, including Justice, who liked a drink in Kehoes before, during, or after the Holy Hour. Vincent being the excellent barman that he was and knowing the strengths and weaknesses of his regular customers, and being a barman 'confidant' of the old school, had a quiet whisper here and there after Regan's troubles were made public, at least in the Civil Service.

Garda McCloy is still Garda McCloy, now unhappily ruling the roost in the station in the Townland of Ballintoor Beg, a suburb so to speak of the village of Ballintoor Mor, wishing he was back in the dizzy and exciting scene in Clones.

Vincent, who nearly smiled on the day, now smiled all the time as he kept busy and paid close attention to all that was important.

Regan continues to count cattle, to this day.

NORA FLEMING
MARTIN SWORDS
PETER HICKEY RUTH
MOORE **J. TED VOIGT**
E. J. RYAN EITHNE
WRIGHT BELINDA
WALSH VERA CAIT
WALSH HELENE
PETERSEN GANESH
RAMACHANDRAN
CAROLANN MURPHY

Joy = mc²

It's a zero-sum business
For art mongers, a joy market
Where those who create
Juice themselves
For their consumers who drink
Up in libraries and galleries
What tax must we pay
To the state
Of mind
What joy is lost due to
Friction of fiction
To the atmospheric metaphor
When joy equals mass times anticipation
And paintings can be arrested
For breaking the first law of thermoemotions.

Baby Girl

We have a lot in common
My baby girl and me
We are both into a few of the same things
Like long walks,
And my wife to name a few.
We both like to be held
We prefer company to solitude
And we both like to eat every 2 hours or so.
Neither one of us likes wet pants
Though there are times
Neither of us can avoid it.
We share several favorite pass-times,
We aspire to be great
And to take great naps.
We like latin music
Because we're trying to improve our Spanish skills
We both like a little milk in the evening
And early in the morning when
Her mom wakes us up
We both stretch out our arms
And vote for snoozing
And now (and this is the best part)
We're a majority

Firmamentalist

Let us seek therefore
Not a foundation but a firmament
Constant and eternal
Yet changing in every moment
Through every season
And from every angle new
Let what is true stand not on cold stone
But lie in wet grass
With backs turned to groundedness
Gazing starward wondering
These Wanderers our founding fathers
These constellations comprise our epistles
For on this earth
We have far too many towers built of stone
Not nearly enough built of stars

Love of Air

It's a love of air
Scandalous but breezy
That keeps us gasping
Grasping for breadth and
Width
Our love of air conditions
Us
Not to dive too deep
Not to burn too hot.
It's a love of air,
Plain and unrequited
Pressing against the insides
Of passionate lungs
Inflated.

NORA FLEMING
MARTIN SWORDS
PETER HICKEY RUTH
MOORE J. TED VOIGT
E. J. RYAN EITHNE
WRIGHT BELINDA
WALSH VERA CAIT
WALSH HELENE
PETERSEN GANESH
RAMACHANDRAN
CAROLANN MURPHY

The Listeners

after the poem by Walter De La Mare

Knock   Knock …..............

Traveller: Is there anybody there....?

Silence (several seconds)

Moon: I don't only reflect the sun's light you know.
                 I watch you though you pay me no heed.
                 Understandable when you consider we've
                 not exchanged a solitary word.

Horse :   Hmmmmph. He's used my four faithful
                 legs to get himself thus far. It's his
                 instincts he'll be needing to travel the final
                 furlong. Until this errand is done I'll just
                 keep you company. Don't mind me while I
                 graze the soft grasses of the forest's ferny
                 floor.

Narrator   A bird flies up out of the turret above,
                 belatedly startled in the darkness. Its
                 solitary shriek pierces the night like a
                 sliver of lightening, then disappears just
                 as quickly back into uncertainty...

Knock Knock ………………….

Traveller :   Is There Anybody There ?!!

Leaves: Oh Hush Hush Hush now Good Sir.
                 We've tickled the sills and the panes with
                 our delicate green veins,

Now just stand back and wait like us,
With usss,
Hussssshhh

Traveller: Reveal yourselves I implore you grey-eyed
phantoms.
Please, Oh Please let us talk.......

Moon: I only wish you might look up..
Allow my sympathy to pour down on
you......
Believe me my good man - you are not
alone...
Not Alone....
You are not alone.

Narrator/Door: The wide-eyed phantoms quiver in
her mysterious watery light,
Luxuriating in it's deathly softness,
Bathing in their removed status,
Never drawing breath.

Traveller : But I am lonely out here.
I fancy I can see you , descending the
stairs,
thronging the hall,
As you were....
As and when we knew each other here
before.

Moon : Allow me to shed further light on your
plight:
Though you may shake and stir the air,
Too much time has passed.
Their strangeness,
Their stillness:
Their answer to your call.

Horse : Dolce, dolce darling moon-
Don't educate him quite so fast,
This grass is delicious.

KNOCK KNOCK KNOCK

Traveller : Tell them that I came and no-one
answered- that I kept my word.

Leaves : It is only we who stir here now.
Listen to our whispers.
We know all too well that you are the only
man left awake.

Traveller : I sense a voice; voices beyond me,
Despite my hopeful wish, the ache in my
heart tells me to leave this place.
It's telling me that nothing stirs within.
Within?

Oh .... Within.

SILENCE (several seconds)

Narrator/Door: His boot slips silently into the
stirrup.
Time for iron to meet stone again.

Horse : Amen . I've had my fill.

Leaves : We told you so.
We told you so.
Leave it to us,
Ours is the job - to softly usher back the
silence when the plunging hoofs
Are gone

Sssssssshhh.

Genesis: What They Do not want You to Know

And in the beginning God said "Let there be Love". Yes friends there we have it: The First Mistake. Beginnings can be such tricky things so it is good, however belatedly so, to correct this error. With this oversight cleared up, life becomes less confusing as other matters fall easily into their right place.

To reiterate, God said "Let there be Love". By seeing with our ears we understand that sound beat light to be the first to reach us from beyond the darkness. This sound being the voice of God Herself, it was no ordinary entrance into the void. It was the food of Love: Music. God later found it necessary to add light merely so that we humans would be able to read the notes.

The rest is history.

Newly Born

The embers of the evening.
A moonlit night
Nine months ago

What impatient passions of spring's tender buds
Crept into your hearts
Without their knowing?

In depth of winter at year's turning
Time ripened fully the pearl and
Stretched the bow of a mother's being

The arrow has left the archer's hands
Life's longing for itself again fulfilled
Let us see how he thrives in the ashes of our lives

For Simon

Fish Eyes

Rise and Fall

First step first fall,
Those eyes,
Fish slab ice,
Those eyes following me, his heart not.
Where warm blood?

Below look up at unknown depths,
Help?
Still silent fish eyes.
Second fall,
Fish slab ice.

Rise,
Third time lucky,
Triumph without trumpets,
Beware those fish eyes.

NORA FLEMING
MARTIN SWORDS
PETER HICKEY **RUTH
MOORE** J. TED VOIGT
E. J. RYAN EITHNE
WRIGHT BELINDA
WALSH VERA CAIT
WALSH HELENE
PETERSEN GANESH
RAMACHANDRAN
CAROLANN MURPHY

Autumn Run

Crisp. Fresh. Nostril hairs tingling.
Cutting. Sharp. Burning sensation.
Piercing. Stabbing. Pressure pot.

Breathing. Rhythm. Keeping pace.
Ragdoll motion. Side-to-side.
Monotonous. Boring. Empty vessel.

Pounding. Stomping. Making ground.
Soft. Uneven. Cushioned landing.
Damp. Wet. Sock soaking.
Home again. Fire burning.

Numbing Love

Nervous hands clenched into timid fists,
Lying arched and still.
His face followed her curve with tongue licks.
As her rigid form relaxed to his will.
His eyes met hers and held a lustful stare
Caught in a rabbit snare.
She closed her eyes before the trap shut
Escaping with only a slight cut.
A cut that would never heal,
Rewounded in first encounters to come.
Getting deeper until she felt no pain at all
Bandaged for a while by some.

NORA FLEMING
MARTIN SWORDS
PETER HICKEY RUTH
MOORE J. TED VOIGT
E. J. RYAN **EITHNE
WRIGHT** BELINDA
WALSH VERA CAIT
WALSH HELENE
PETERSEN GANESH
RAMACHANDRAN
CAROLANN MURPHY

A Tribute to Poets

Writers of verse
I greatly admire
Gifted with imaginative talent
Converting time and place
Raising them to a different planet.

Breaking down barriers
Uplifting our horizons
Bringing harmony to language
Satisfying the senses.

A poet communicates to others
Pictures of their own internal thoughts
Of the ever changing rhythms of life,
From the sorrowful to the sublime.

A poem, like a mirror
Enhances the mundane
Transforming the ordinary
Lifting a veil to reveal
The hidden beauty of this world.

An Ode to Love

Love, oh welcome malady
From which no one seeks a cure
Afflicting the young and even the more mature
Striking the unsuspecting
Anywhere, anytime
At a bus stop, in a lift, or on a train.

Oh the thrill, the quickened pulse
The rapid heart rate
The longing for – the expectation of
This delicious agony usurps our peace of mind
Leaving us restless lovesick victims in a bind.

Love unrequited must surely end in pain
The jilted lover weeps, depressed
The object of his love may treat him with disdain
Yet he must take heart and not complain
For this malady is wont to strike again and again.

Clouds

Swirls of cloud scurrying across the sky
Great mounds of cotton wool
Harmless, masking the brightness beneath.

Then darkening, threatening, assuming different shapes
Some like giant boulders
Others animal like, fearsome, menacing, grotesque monsters
Harbingers of rough weather to come
Always moving, changing, merging, embracing.

Filaments of white and grey
Wispy, thread-like – benign
Some leading the posse
Others isolated from the pack making singular statements
Then vanishing from sight.

Reflecting life – how it invades and strangles us
Interjecting on our lives
Bringing sadness, even despair
Leaving us vanquished, crushed, bewildered and forlorn.

Patience then, hold fast
This grief like the clouds will become dislodged
Out of the gloom and pockets of darkness
Black boulders dissipate
A ray of light breaks in upon the gloom
The sun comes out – the storm has passed.

Francis Bacon (The solitary poet)

Untutored in his art
Yet causing a sensation at the Tate
With his Crucifixion figures.

His subjects – Gloomy in nature
Distorted human forms
Representations of pain and agony
Emphasizing the evils of man.

Studio clutter gives us a clue
He admits it is a mess
Likening it to his anguished state of mind
From whence dark thoughts emerge.

The artist – so unsure of his gift
The hesitation – paintings untitled – unfinished
A lament for his inadequacy:
"I tend to destroy the better ones"

Evoking our regret for that lost art.
Then let us appreciate him all the more.

Late Date

I.

It was getting late. I parted the net curtains and looked out on to the damp street. Still no sign. "Nonsense. Of course he'll turn up" said my mother. " You said he was a nice guy. He might have to close the shop himself – a staff member might have to go home early. He's bound to keep his word and wasn't it your friend who introduced you?"

"Hey, wait a minute! Whose word? How important is this anyway? Why should this be such a crucial event in my life whether or not he turns up? So what if I was stood up twice? I'll get over it. No one ever died of a broken heart after being jilted. Mum, that friend of yours who said her sister did – that's rubbish. I bet there was coronary heart disease in her family. She pined for her boyfriend when he was away in the army. He came home and was a different person. I'll bet he was. He fancied a different girl. More fool she".

Honestly, though it was awful that evening – I was standing there like an idiot in my high heels watching all the couples meeting. The joy on their faces, the eager expectation of an enjoyable evening to come. Some had theatre tickets. Others pored over the evening paper wondering what film to see – discussing actors, plots, etc. Whenever they looked my way I fumbled in my handbag. Well I could have a car and be looking for my keys. People don't search for their keys entering a car park. They might be set upon.

Looking back, I should never have listened to the girls in the office. " Bowl him over" they said. This new hairstyle does not suit me. My face is too long for such a short haircut. He probably came, had a peek and buzzed off or he could have brought his pals and said,

"Would ye look at your wan?"

They say if possible date a friend or a friend of a friend. That way you can check on his C.V. 15,20, 30 minutes went by. My goodness I must be hard up to have waited so long in the cold before I got out of there and went in search of Nuala the friend I always turn to and who would listen to a hard luck story. You'd never go to your own with this kind of trouble.

I need to give myself a good talking to. Who wants marriage nowadays? Unmarried people have everything going for them, freedom, holidays when they choose, do what they like with their money and have time to cultivate friendships and hobbies. They don't have to cater for mood swings or worry about business deals going wrong or apologise for their actions and I would never be a candidate as a de facto wife.

Hey, I ask you – whose wishes are at stake here. I swear I'm allowing myself to be conditioned. It's alright for my mother to promote marriage. It worked for her. That is no guarantee it would work for me. "I don't want any old maids in this family" she preached and my two sisters kindly obliged by giving her two great days out. Two of my best friends are back in the office after separation. It's great they can console each other. I worked jolly hard to get where I am. I went to night classes and studied for my qualification in Public Administration. It was a hard graft and then having to face Jack Cuthbert in the morning. He was not well pleased after being passed over for promotion by a woman. Well patriarchy has been waked long ago.

2.
No! I'll never again risk getting a cold standing under Clery's clock waiting for a man. That is why I told this bloke to call for me at my house.

So what if he has my address? He can add it to all the rest and the telephone numbers of the girls he made dates with.

My whole happiness does not depend on the whim of a mere male. It won't cause an international incident if he goes out with his mates instead. Anyway what trainee supermarket manager owns a BMW unless he has wealthy parents and there are not many of them around. So much for dating a friend of a friend!

"Listen I hear a car turning" my mother said. She drew the curtains again and left them parted. One glance, and there by the street light I saw him – a stunning figure in a dark suit and wearing a white shirt. He was ringing the bell at the house next door.

"Mum, don't open the door immediately he rings. Let him wait. I have to finish putting on my make-up. And Mum, those library books I brought you are on the hall table. Don't wait up. I'll let myself in. Who cares who owns the car? I always liked only the best".

P.S.   We were married two years later.

Lucia's Dilemma

Words, Words, Words
Too many Words overwhelm
I've grown weary of syntax
And of marshalling words.

Father, if you were a salesman
And not a Wordsmith
Life would be simpler
Our joy less constrained.

Now I want to be free
To dance with Diagheliv
And the Grisettes in the Moulon Rouge
Ride bareback in the Circus.

I feel empty, desolate
My lover has left me
Darkness surrounds me
Would someone please rescue me!

Parody on a Yeats Poem

I will arise and go now
To park my car beside Bank C.
That once hallowed institution
Where people lodged their money
For perfect safety.

Instead of thrift, bankers lent our money recklessly
They consorted with developers, men in Mercs. and Four by
Fours
Who built high rise apartment blocks
And houses by the score.

Cranes rose high into the sky
Casting shadows on the streets
No complaints were uttered
The aim was double digit growth.

Men in builders' suits and hats
Were busy building blocks
Sales in breakfast rolls and take-aways began to soar and soar
All were celebrating the Celtic Tiger's roar.

Yet there were those who feared our little Isle
Could no longer be called green
Masses of grey concrete everywhere was seen.

An outbreak of property mania then took hold
Many citizens became obsessed
Brought on by record house sales
At prices far exceeding their worth.

But there were some who feared disaster
And foretold a day of doom
They were dismissed as spoil sports all
So the people partied on.

The Bankers couldn't sleep one night

And came knocking on the Minister's door
They said the money was all gone
And brazenly asked for more.

But none returned their bonuses
They just promised to make amends.

Security Guards were hired at Bankers' A.G.M.'s
To control the angry mob
But one irate investor let fly with eggs
And almost hit one in the gob.

Now it's cutbacks and tightened belts
To compensate for past excesses
And made to measure hairshirts can be had
At bargain basement prices

Yet, this may be beneficial for the nation
If it produces a more lean and fit generation.

Some agree there yet may be a general uprising
But I advise against this course
It might foment upheaval
The Troica might have their headphones on
And listening to an R.E. Station.

Better to live within our means
Just as our parents did of old
Until our Balance Sheet's in the black
And a return to fiscal creditation.

The Space Inside My Head

I.
Countless facts accumulated
Thousands processed
I keep adding to the list
But now I'm starting to forget
Which makes me quite upset
Fearing there's no more space inside my head.

I've got the essentials
That should suffice
But the nagging persists
There's much more to be known
But how can I measure how much space is left.

To solve my dilemma
I've thought of a plan
To dispense with irrelevant and useless information
As much as I can
Eliminate the negative
And retain only positive facts instead.

To acquire a new wavelength
May be the answer
Though it might necessitate wearing a hat
But if it would solve my problem
I'm prepared for that
Then I could store more facts
Gleaned from gossip and chit chat
But if the hat became sodden and the batteries went flat
Communication would cease even wearing a new hat.

I've tried to resist engaging in small talk
But my resolve is weakening
The temptation's too strong
I can only hold out for so long
As I must hear the latest instalment
Of my friend's on/off romance.

The solution might be a device attached to my ear
To filter the data and monitor what I hear
And give an accurate reading of the vacant space left in my
head
But if I'm not in charge
Some items might pass

2.
Of which I'd disapprove
And others I'd like might be consigned to the trash
That's where a reject button would come into play
Then I myself would have the last say.

And if my discovery should prove a success
I'd be interviewed on T.V. and pictured in the Press
I might even become famous when I market my design
Then all monetary rewards would be mine.

Oh the glory, the ultimate satisfaction!
Of being the first to invent a brand new contraption.

NORA FLEMING
MARTIN SWORDS
PETER HICKEY RUTH
MOORE J. TED VOIGT
E. J. RYAN EITHNE
WRIGHT BELINDA
WALSH **VERA CAIT
WALSH** HELENE
PETERSEN GANESH
RAMACHANDRAN
CAROLANN MURPHY

A Gentle Soul

A gentle soul.
Timid, afraid,
yet brave,
when passions roused.

Easy toward love,
and easily loved.
Like an inner light
on a cold, dark night.

I knew her,
not by name.
A presence floating by
adding colour to my life.

Her eyes were kind,
and with a smile
she listened,
all the while I spoke.

A gentle soul,
timid, afraid,
yet, brave,
Armed with love.

New Year's Night

I watch the sky
explode with light,
as I stand alone
on New Year's night

Splendid colours
of red and blue,
yellow too
Illuminate my view

Memories of another eve
add sadness to my eyes.
Yet, resolute, I take delight
in the splendour of
New Year's night.

Safe Haven

Waiting at the door
of tranquillity,
I watch the moving traffic
as it flows, like bright lights
of independent gods.

I wonder at the speed
that drives our human race.
Can we conceive
a world of calm and peace
in this fast-track place?

I step inside the door
and marvel at the silence,
away from noise and strife
in this hidden
'other' life.

With gladness, I relax
in the wisdom of a choice
that opens ancient doors
into a forgotten place
of solitude,
where even gods repose.

A World of Trees

In Glenmalure,
this sacred place
lies a graveyard
of depleted trees.
Nature spoiled,
man beguiled
by need.

Must we change
the world?
Or can we
take solace
in a sacred code
that provides,
not for our wants,
just for our needs.

The Bridge

I stand on the bridge
and watch.
Like stairs of water,
the river cascades down
the mountain-side.

I look down
over the swelling torrent
as the river gushes
and rushes
carrying all in its way.

I could let the river
make my course.
Let me flow
with excited spirit
into the valley below.

Or, I could stay
on this fragile bridge.
Remain between choices,
pondering,
will I stay or go?

Would this be wrong?
Can we not play
at being who we are.
People, fragile,
afraid to move on.

Solace by the Sea

I watch, entranced
by the rhythm of crashing
slashing waves and
shingle song.

The sea, like a hungry,
restless giant
taunts me closer,
to the edge.

A show of strength
from a gentle God,
invites in me a state
of calm tranquillity.

When I am weak,
perhaps I'm also strong
Just like my God
upon a wave-swept song.

Sunshine

Vitamin D they say,
essential for the body
and a healthy mind.

Vitamin D can be
bought in bottles
from any store in town.

Yet, I believe
in sunshine, warm
and pleasing to the eye.

Sunshine on my body
causing me to glow
and shine with vitality

Sunshine comes in bottles
for those who want to fake
For me, in Gran Canary
is the sunshine that I seek.

Filler

There was a time
when I would reach
for mountains; climb them
when I could.

I'd reach up to the sky
and wonder why
my feet were still united
to the ground.

Now, I find my place
in life to be a 'filler'
Someone who is there
to mend a patch, or fill a hole.

Time has taught me how
to reach for little things
for pleasures one so
easily forgets,

Listening to a friend,
Sharing laughter,
Standing in for those
who need a rest.

No glory in the role
of being a filler
Just a remedy for cracks
in human kind.

I use a trowel
packed with humour
Smooth it off
as only love can do.

Happy are my thoughts
as I move along the years

adding moral mortar
here and there.

When my time comes to go
I'll be ready
to add an extra touch
to God's sweet plan.

The Man

I think of God
As if He were a man
Someone who dares to care
A Person there, for everyone.

This Person, this Man
Is bold and brave, never afraid
His banner bears the imprint
of honesty.

A Man of integrity.
Able to speak His mind
Yet compassionate to all mankind
Someone I so easily can love.

I dare to say His name
Invite Him, in my ignorance,
To be a part of me
He willingly complies,
We become as one.

Cafe Chatter

Two women, serving in a small Cafe, are preparing tea for customers.

ELLIE   Mona, did you see that?

MONA   See what?

ELLIE   The two in the corner... the love-birds.

MONA   Them? Those two old ones?
Love-birds? Ellie, you're losing it...

ELLIE   (Whispering) Keep your voice down.
Would you shut up and watch.

SILENCE

ELLIE   See!
Did you see that?

MONA   Didn't see anythin...
Oh, you mean the card on the table?

ELLIE   Yea... Oh Mona, it's awful romantic.

MONA   It's just a card.

ELLIE   It's a Valentine card!

MONA   You can see that from here?

ELLIE   I peeked at it, when I brought over
the tea.

MONA   God, they're awful old to be...
you know...

ELLIE   Oh, look look... (whispering)... discreetly.
Don't stare.
He's holding her hand.

Ellie gives a deep sigh...

ELLIE   If only I had someone like that.

MONA   (Giggling) You have your other-half at
home.

ELLIE   I know. My George, God bless him...
Hasn't a romantic bone in his body.

MONA   At least you have a man.

ELLIE   Mona, you're better off without that
good-for-nothing.
If he ever comes near you again...

MONA   He won't. He's skipped off to England.
Soon as the Judge said he'd have to
support the kids... disappeared the very
next day.

ELLIE   I never liked him, Mona....

CRASH!

ELLIE   Oh Lord, them young ones' smashed a
cup...
(To people) Hold on, I'll get a cloth...

Ellie goes over and wipes up the mess...

ELLIE   (To old couple) Sorry for the
disturbance...

They smile at her...

ELLIE   (Back with Mona) I saw the card.
                 Lovely hand-written poem inside.

MONA   I got one of them Valentine cards once,
                 long time ago.
                 Didn't do me much good.

ELLIE   (Distracted) Would you look...
                 He's reading out the poem to her.

MONA   Did you ever get one?

ELLIE   A Valentine card? No, never.
                 No romance in my George.
                 Still, he did marry me.

MONA   Ellie, he kissed her hand!
                 Imagine that...

ELLIE   Yea, imagine that.

The old couple get up. She leaves first.
He comes over to pay...

ELLIE   Ah, that's alright sir.
                 Today's a special day.

He smiles and leaves the Cafe.
Mona watches after him...

MONA   Ellie, isn't that strange...

ELLIE   What's strange?

MONA   Them love-birds...
                 They went in opposite directions...
                 They weren't together at all.

ELLIE   Fancy that!

5 Minute Radio Play

The setting is the backyard of a suburban home. RALF and
DOLLY are relaxing on the grass, enjoying the sunshine.

RALF   Now, this is what I call LIFE!

DOLLY   Yea... have to agree with you there.
PAUSE
How was work today?

RALF   Rough...
Dolly, I don't know if I can handle it,
anymore...

Dolly moves closer to him; gives him a friendly nudge.

DOLLY   Ralf, you mustn't say things like that. You...
you're one of the best...

RALF   (Butting in) And the oldest. Those others...
cheeky pups... try to undermine my authority...

DOLLY   Don't pay attention to them. Their ignorance
will trip them up, just wait and see...

She gently rubs her sleek body against his as she moves closer
to him on the grass.

DOLLY   Pay attention to me. I'll soothe your troubles
away.

Ralf snuggles closer to her

RALF   What would I do without you...

Suddenly, a dark shadow descends upon them, blotting out the
sunlight...

DOLLY   (Whimpering) It... it's gotten cold...

RALF   It's him... he's here, again...

DOLLY   (Frightened) Oh Ralf, I'm afraid...

RALF   (Comforting) Don't be. I'll protect you.

Ralf leaps up and barks loudly at the fat boy; snarling and attempting to bite him... The fat boy lifts his boot and sends Ralf flying across the yard, senseless.

BOY   Hah! Stupid dog...

He suddenly screams with pain as Dolly sinks her teeth into his rear-end, tearing his trousers and leaving teeth-marks on his flesh. He rushes off, crying. Dolly runs over to Ralf who is lying in a daze on the grass.

DOLLY   Ralf... darling. Are you alright?

RALF   Oh Dolly, you are my hero!

Limping, he snuggles close to her sleek coat as they march off into the sunset.

ENDS..

APPROX. 2 MINS.

Impressions

In and out, all about
constant in its flow.
Reverently, I gaze
at the sea below.

Pebbles, brown and grey
unique in their array
wait for the sea
to polish their display.

Silhouette of sun,
through a sky of grey
adds hope
to yet another day.

My cares are put aside,
let this moment be.
Watch the changing tide,
listen to the music of the sea.

NORA FLEMING
MARTIN SWORDS
PETER HICKEY RUTH
MOORE J. TED VOIGT
E. J. RYAN EITHNE
WRIGHT BELINDA
WALSH VERA CAIT
WALSH HELENE
PETERSEN **GANESH**
RAMACHANDRAN
CAROLANN MURPHY

The Roadettes

The beginning of the first episode of a television comedy drama series

EXT. STREET - DAY

SUPER: 1975

A brightly coloured scooter, the name NINA emblazoned on the side, In the saddle, Nina grins, waves. VERA, also riding a similar scooter, joins Nina at the road junction, and the two ride abreast, smiling at each other. COLEEN emerges on scooter from a side road, waving. All three ride, side-by-side.

EXT. A PUBLIC (DRINKING) HOUSE – DAY

The three girls park outside and disembark. Inside, guitars can be heard in the style of 1950s rock and roll music.

INT. PUBLIC HOUSE BAR - DAY

The bar is full of drinkers (PUNTERS). They are somewhat boisterous. The three girls enter the bar, and they are greeted with wolf-whistles.

A musical band is tuning up. The band comprises of an 'ELVIS' lookalike, 'CLIFF' Richard lookalike, and a drummer (PHIL). 'ELVIS' and 'CLIFF' are on guitars.

The PUB LANDLORD enters the bar.

PUB LANDLORD:Alright, you punters. Settle Down. As usual for your delectation, we've got the Kings of Rock and Roll, Elvis the King himself, and our own pretender Cliff Richard...and oh yeah, their backing singers.

The group is given sleazy cheers and claps from the Punters.

CLIFF: C'mon girls, we haven't got all day.

NINA: So what one we doing?

ELVIS: Jailhouse Rock.

COLEEN: Jaysus no, I can't get them high notes.

VERA: Too many cigarettes Coleen, that's your problem.

Vera, Nina and Coleen line up behind 'Elvis' and 'Cliff'. The two guys sing, backed by the three girls, in the chorus.

Partway through the song, 'Cliff' stops singing.

CLIFF: Hey, that was my bit!

ELVIS: Shut-up. Elvis is King,

CLIFF: I've had enough of this! I quit.

'Cliff' storms off.

ELVIS: I quit too. Come on, Phil!

'Phil' and 'Elvis' walk off, leaving the girls centre-stage, and sheepish.

A LONG HAIRED PUNTER from the audience shouts out.

A LONG HAIRED: Show us your Shangri-La's, darlings!

Embarrased, the girls scuttle away.

EXT. STREET - NIGHT

VERA: I think we've been sacked! Temperamental old crows, those two singers, I could see it coming though.

NINA: Elvis versus Cliff, all over again!

COLEEN: I really enjoyed the crack of it. Sure what else is there to do around here?

VERA: Maybe some other guys will let us sing in their band.

NINA: We've tried that so many times, and they just dump us when they feel like. We need to move on.

Vera, Nina and Coleen mount their scooters, very upset. They drive up the road and head their separate ways.

INT: NINA'S HOUSE -NIGHT

MR. PRICE and MRS. PRICE, watch TV. The 'Yorkshire Television' logo and tune appear.

Television Voiceover
It's Sunday Night! So now, from Scarborough, Northern Star! Ten new talents battle it out-

Nina arrives home, glimpsing the TV. Mrs. Price promptly turns it off.

MRS. PRICE: Nina...sit down, We need to talk to you. You can't ruin your job at the Bank by hanging out with those girls.

NINA: But they are my best friends!

MRS PRICE: Your father has always had a safe job at the bank, Thirty years, father?

MR PRICE: Yes, mother.

NINA: Sorry, but I don't want to spend the rest of my life behind a counter giving out fivers and stamping a ledger.

MRS PRICE: The impudence, Nina! Tell her off father!

MR PRICE: Yes, mother. The impudence, Nina!

MRS PRICE: We want you to meet some nice boys. Tarquin, the Bank manager's son likes you.

NINA: He's not very exciting.

MRS PRICE: Your father was not very exciting. But I married him. Did I not, father?

MR PRICE: Yes, Mother I mean, no, mother.

MRS PRICE: Okay, if you like socialisation, how about the bank dining club?

NINA: It's very boring. People just talk about the Bank. I like to sing, I like to paint.

MRS PRICE: There's the Bank Arts Club.

NINA: They are all over seventy in there, past it!

MRS PRICE: Your contemptuous attitude...The Bank would not stand for your cheek, young lady. Father tell her off!

MR PRICE   Yes mother. The con..contemp...Bank.

NINA: Bank, Bank, Bank, that's all I hear, day in and day out.

Nina storms off.

INT. COLEEN'S COUNCIL HOUSE - NIGHT

LIAM minds baby AGNETHA, She cries loudly and wriggles.

Coleen storms into the front room.

COLEEN: Da, I showed you how to feed Agnetha, change her, wind her.

LIAM: It's not my job to be looking after your babbie. Where is it's father. Anyway she's fine.

COLEEN: Fine? Her bum's the colour of daddies sauce, so it is.

LIAM: So what happened? You said an extra hour.

COLEEN: We got the sack. Given us the heave-ho. Go out there and get a job.

LIAM: That's no way to talk to your brother When you came over from Donegal, you never said you were pregnant.

COLEEN: What other reason was there to leave the village, you thick arse!

LIAM: What man would have you now?

COLEEN: Singing has given me more satisfaction than any man, so it has.

LIAM: And more than your baby?

Coleen is silent and pensive.

INT. VERA'S FLAT - NIGHT

RON pushes open the main door and staggers into the house.

VERA: What time do you call this, Ron?

RON: Vera. Vera, Vera. My sweetness and light, I've come home to make love to you.

VERA: You reckon? It'd be a first.

RON: You're all I need darling.

VERA: You're passionless until you have a bit of drink in you, then you're about as useful as Basil's brush!

Ron collapses onto the sofa into a drunken stupor.

INT. NINA'S BEDROOM - NIGHT

Nina's 'Blue Peter Badge' presentation pack sits on her bedside table. Nina looks through a book of press cuttings featuring Robin with herself, Vera and Coleen. In the background, there is a radio documentary about fifties/early sixties girl singers and bands.

Nina lies back on her bed, listening.

MRS PRICE: (from downstairs)   It's nearly ten o'clock, turn the lights out and go to bed young lady!

Music; 'You Don't Own Me' by Lesley Gore.

VOICE ON THE RADIO: Who can forget, Martha and the Vandellas, the Shangri-Las...

Time passes, as Nina listens to more girl singers, and Nina begins to drift off.

VOICE ON THE RADIO: ...and then of course 'The Ronettes'. Were they one hit wonders? Or was their star yet to shine?

Nina's painting stand has a blank sheet on the canvas. There is a stack of paints and pencils next to the stand. Nina wakes up with a start. She grabs her pencils and starts sketching.

MONTAGE:

Nina paints the sketch, at night. Nina works at the bank by day, handing out money and stamping the ledger, frustrated.

Vera works in the betting shop by day, dealing with men cheekily chatting her up. Nina continues to paint the same picture at night.

Coleen, with Agnetha, collects unemployment benefit, There are disapproving looks from people in the benefits office, who whisper comments to each other with reference to her single mother status.

Vera has fierce arguments with her drunken, mellow husband in their flat at night. Coleen cleans toilets in the pub by night, and gets 'cash in hand'. Nina continues to paint her picture at night. She smiles in satisfaction that it's complete.

END MONTAGE.

NORA FLEMING
MARTIN SWORDS
PETER HICKEY RUTH
MOORE J. TED VOIGT
E. J. RYAN EITHNE
WRIGHT BELINDA
WALSH VERA CAIT
WALSH HELENE
PETERSEN GANESH
RAMACHANDRAN
CAROLANN MURPHY

A Letter Came Today

Helen's hands tightened on the steering wheel as she got nearer and nearer the turn for Rowan Drive in Deansgrange. "Get a grip she said to herself, but not such a tight one "- she gave a slight laugh. Before turning into the estate she almost knocked a cyclist down – "really now Helen, this is not funny at all." The last five hours she played her CDs and daydreamed about the last three weeks, the best summer ever with her family in Ballyconnelly – she was beginning to wish she had taken up their offer to stay for the last week but....on the other hand...her thoughts drifted........

Pulling into No 30, her hands were shaking now, and a headache materialised from nowhere, the beginning of a migraine. Instead of going straight in she turned off the engine and lit up a cigarette. Exactly four weeks ago today...it all played out again before her - opening the door and two men standing there, taking up the whole door frame.. We are Gardai ("yeah I can see that by your hats" she remembers thinking) from Blackrock Station, and you must be Mrs Ham. Before she could utter "never heard of her" the slightly smaller one said, "it's about your husband David ...("oh yes, now I remember I AM Mrs Ham"), we have very bad news- he died earlier today following a one vehicle car crash in Co. Meath". The cigarette burned into her finger and the ashes went all over her top – wake up Helen and get on with the day, this is all past tense.

Before unpacking the car she went inside and on the floor she found a pile of post, brown envelopes - she hated those ones - some junk and at the very bottom a blue envelope with handwriting – she picked it up and there it was Mr David R Ham, 30 Rowan Drive - no senders address on the back. She was tempted to bin it but then decided no "what the heck I better have a look." Inside was a letter, from someone who obviously knew David well AND that he had married recently - well 18 months ago, and knew Helen's name. The final paragraph took her by surprise - "so James, the kids and myself will be in the Radisson on Friday, 28th August and we would love to meet you both, say around 4pm. David and Rhiannon are really looking forward to seeing you, David, after all these years." The letter was signed "Wendy".

Helen was thrown into a spin, the 28th was that very day and she reckoned they must have sent this letter weeks ago – Wendy did not date the letter and the postmark was smudged. Questions flew around her brain – "had they heard yet that David was dead?" and the biggest one of all - "who are they"? David never mentioned anyone called Wendy – he had one brother in London called Cedric, his aunt Nan and her husband Wilf who brought Cedric and himself up when their mother died. A cousin possibly, or a neighbour from Cardiff where he lived?

There really was no time to waste, Helen decided to have a quick wash and change and to head for the Radisson, just in time for the afternoon 'reunion.'

The Radisson was packed when she arrived, and it dawned on her that she had no idea what this family looked like. She found a good seat though where she could watch the crowd and maybe spot some people looking around for a complete stranger. Shortly, however, she heard a voice from across the bar, "Helen, Helen, I'm over here". So, it seemed that Wendy had a photo of David and herself, sent by David some months beforehand. Wendy had kept some seats and ushered Helen over to her table, with explanations that James and the kids would be along shortly.

Wendy looked around and of course Helen realised that she was looking for David. She felt dizzy, her palms were sweaty and her throat had gone completely dry. There was no other option but to blurt it straight out "I am sorry about this news but David was killed in a car crash, four weeks ago". The strangest thing, but Helen thought she saw a slight smile in Wendy's eyes for a split second, but then maybe not. Wendy reached for her bag and took out a packet of Bensen and Hedges. The waiter was going around and she called him over, "a large gin and tonic please and you Helen?" " Oh same for me" Helen said. As Helen recounted the events of four weeks ago, a man, James it would seem, approached the table with two children, laughing and punching each other.

It was Helen's turn to 'smile slightly and then go to jelly' because the boy was an exact replica of David, her dead husband – the same sparkly smiling eyes, sallow skin, black hair – just the same, it was impossible to quantify it.

Wendy allowed a quick hello from the children, David and Rhiannon, and then asked James to take them out into the gardens while she talked to Helen.

Wendy told Helen the whole story then, right from the beginning – her marriage to David when they were students, the two children David and Rhiannon and the eventual divorce. The children had not seen their father for five years at least but when she heard that David had settled down she thought it might be a good time to make the connection again. Suddenly, Wendy said "what was he doing in Co. Meath"? and Helen had to tell her that she had no idea. " A man of many secrets still, Helen, and the worlds worst womanizer!!!" Helen could not argue with Wendy because the details in her story were so familiar to her, even though she had not yet come to terms with the man she married, twelve years older than her and a stranger now it seems.

Shortly after Helen made her excuses to leave, explaining that she was exhausted from the long trip from Connemara. Wendy would have to explain events to her new husband, James, and the children – she simply could not face this ordeal. On her way out of Rowan Drive earlier she noticed Joseph her postman going in her gateway – and for once hoped it was one of those boring brown envelopes.

In another twenty minutes she was opening the front door in number 30 Rowan Drive and she found herself staring at the floor in the hallway. A letter came today. It had a white envelope this time, and was addressed to Monsiour David R Ham – from Madame Maria Perriquet , Chateau Lamote, Haux, near Bordeaux on the back. She placed the letter behind the clock on the mantelpiece and lit up a cigarette. Without thinking she kicked off her shoes, and threw herself on the couch. Helen had enough excitement to last her for a long, long time.

Mates for Life

Who are those wild black and white beauties
Gliding silently over seascape?
On ground, in colony high pitched cackling
Ascending and descending in hysterical revelry
At Skellig Michael, one of their remotest homes

A chorus of storm petrels chirp a lullaby
For the waiting chick, safe in its burrow.
Pacing – no, more waddling on fragments of discarded shell
For the return of mother, or father to groom and feed

Once, annihilated by a pack of marauding, shipwrecked rats
On its native Isle of Man
The Manx Shearwater, a survivor, back again
Male and female birds, sharing the load
And... mates for life.

NORA FLEMING
MARTIN SWORDS
PETER HICKEY RUTH
MOORE J. TED VOIGT
E. J. RYAN EITHNE
WRIGHT BELINDA
WALSH VERA CAIT
WALSH **HELENE**
PETERSEN GANESH
RAMACHANDRAN
CAROLANN MURPHY

Blockage

It is here – that numb, dead feeling of nothing
Creative nothing – could let the world in perhaps
But not willing to risk the possibility of everyday life taking
over
as it so often does

Reality took over this past week
My boss is becoming a certified presence in my life
More real, more human, more boss
My friend with all her baggage became more real and very
human
needing a friend, someone who won't judge

So there it is, reality has kicked in and invaded my thoughts
Thank you fellow writers for this meeting
Words in tones, volumes, voices
Your words, your tones in volumes, your voices

Words are flowing from this pen
Not sure if they have really connected in my brain
Before reaching the pen
Could this be a magic pen?

The pen
The mediator between reality and the point where I let it go
The point where the words flow
Writer or not
Words that encompass and become my world
Where reality changes its voice, form, meaning and significance

Thank you fellow lovers of words and dreams
Thank you pen
Reality – see you in the present and the future
When a new story will begin

NORA FLEMING
MARTIN SWORDS
PETER HICKEY RUTH
MOORE J. TED VOIGT
E. J. RYAN EITHNE
WRIGHT **BELINDA
WALSH** VERA CAIT
WALSH HELENE
PETERSEN GANESH
RAMACHANDRAN
CAROLANN MURPHY

The Dreaded Drive Home

Andrew Flynn's 6ft. frame shrunk on seeing his fifteen year old daughter, dragging her bag through the arrivals hall at the airport. The last passenger, this pale faced waif with panda eyes wearing a tatty, grey sweatshirt and black skinny jeans looked like the ghost of the pretty girl he had seen off to school two months earlier. She glanced wearily in his direction but made no sign of recognition. Andrew took a deep breath as he walked towards the small girl and took her gently by the shoulders. "For God's sake Angelina, what is wrong with you? Are you ill or something?"

"Thanks a lot, so nice to see you too," she mumbled, shrugging him off and walking away in disgust. Andrew felt his patience disappear. Angelina was displaying one hell of an attitude he thought, for someone who had just been expelled from school for drinking alcohol. "Ok, young lady," he said catching up with her and taking hold of her arm. "It's this way to the car park. We'll talk there and you have some explaining to do." As Angelina climbed into the car Andrew noticed the tip of a packet of Marlboro in the back pocket of her jeans. He threw her bag impatiently into the back seat of the car and sat heavily into the driver's seat. "So this is what you're up to now, drinking and smoking!" he said, gripping the steering wheel, aware that he was failing to sound as calm, as he had planned. Angelina stroked the dashboard. "Nice new car, Dad. A Mercedes no less...impresses the girlfriend, does it?" "What?" Andrew said in disbelief, turning to face his daughter. "What's going on here Angelina? Let's talk about you drinking in school?" He asked with some authority in his voice. Angelina gave her Dad a quick furtive glance. "It was just a few beers and anyway what do you care?" she said sarcastically. Andrew felt tired. "What makes you think I don't care Angelina?" his voice was almost a whisper. Her eyes flashed at him angrily, "stop it, stop pretending you care, it's so obvious you don't want me around," she yelled. "You want me out of the way, that's why you packed me off to boarding school, so that you could be with your new women. You've forgotten all about Mum. I hate you." Andrew couldn't respond. Her words struck him like stones to his heart. Who was this girl? Where had his gentle, loving daughter gone? His little angel. They had always been so close. He had never seen her have an outburst like this before. When Angelina looked at her father again his face looked pained and crumbled as if all the air had been kicked out of his body. Seeing him like this, knowing she was hurting the person she loved most in the world, felt like agony and she turned her head to allow her tears to flow unseen.

How had things gotten this bad between them? Andrew wondered. How had he messed up so much? He hadn't been aware of how much she was suffering. He had been so wrapped up in his own grief. Eventually he found the words, "I'm not trying to get rid of you, Angel. I'm very sorry you feel that way, I love you very much." he said placing his hand on hers. "Don't touch me," she snapped, pulling her hand away. The pain in her dark brown eyes squeezed at his heart. He was filled with sadness and regret for not being there for her. He couldn't say another word for fear of breaking down. He hadn't cried since May's funeral two years ago. He had done his best to block it all out with work and other distractions but there it was, he realised, all that raw pain just under the surface. Father and daughter sat staring into their own dark caverns of sadness, both exhausted and lost for words. A heavy silence fell between them. Eventually, Andrew turned on the ignition and they started their long journey home. The continuous lights of oncoming traffic had a hypnotic effect on Angelina and she soon dosed off. Andrew glanced at his sleeping daughter from time to time and was struck by how like her mother she had become. They had the same strong profile, dark eyebrows and straight nose. Maybe some part of him had pushed her away because she reminded him of May. "I'm so sorry, May" he whispered. "Forgive me for not looking after our little girl, God help me May, I can't do this without you, I miss you so much." His tears began to blur his vision so he pulled into a lay-by and turned off the engine. In the silence, a tsunami of grief poured out of him and his thoughts went to the night of the accident. He remembered the deafening screech of brakes and relived again the seconds of pure terror just before impact. Inside the car, it felt like they were being hit by a stampeding herd of elephants, dense, powerful and unstoppable. He would never forget the choking smell of gasoline and burnt rubber and the eerie sounds of twisted metal in the dark as he held his wife's head in his hands as she died. A large truck had smashed in the passenger side of their car, killing May in minutes and leaving Angelina and him with just minor injuries. Now, in the same darkness he cried out his anger and his pain and the guilt he felt at being alive. "Oh! May, it should have been me who died...not you. Our daughter needs you, I don't know what to do, how to help her. I'm useless without you." With gratitude Andrew looked at Angelina sleeping soundly beside him and thanked God, she hadn't seen him falling apart like this. "I don't want to lose you too" he whispered through his tears. He watched the small stirrings behind her smudged eyelids and noticed a slight smile on her lips as she dreamt. She is so young, still just a child, he thought and he began to feel a sense of relief. There was plenty of time to turn this around, he told himself. From now on, he promised to do his utmost to be a better father to her. Two hours later Angelina awoke to the familiar sound of car wheels crunching on the gravel of their driveway and to Toby barking in the distance. "We're home at last." Andrew said turning to face his daughter. "I'm sorry Angel, I haven't been here for you. I've been so selfish but I promise you things are going to be different from now on." To his surprise Angelina leaned into him for a hug. "It's ok Dad, I'm sorry too. I was really dreading this drive home but everything is going to be ok. I had a lovely dream of Mum. She said I have to help you and if we both look after each other we will be fine." At that, Angelina opened the car door to greet an excited Labrador running towards them. Standing on his driveway Andrew felt taller and lighter. He stopped to listen to the gentle rustle of leaves in the trees and looking up he saw that the sky was awash with bright stars. Filled with a sense of wonder and gratitude he whispered to the heavens, "Thank you, May."

Golden Moments

A low, painful groan, raw and animal like, silenced us. Joan hurried to her son, lying on a mattress on the kitchen floor, to make him comfortable. Her only child, nineteen year old Stephen was severely mentally and physically handicapped. At six feet, two inches, the boy was a long, lean contortion of painful limbs that had been operated on thirteen times so far. Saddened by the harsh reality of their lives, I turned to watch the ever changing Irish sky through the kitchen window. Dark, swelling clouds made me long for my sun washed home in Southern California. I wanted to scoop them both up and take them there that instant. "He's comfortable now" Joan said returning a few minutes later with a fresh pot of tea. "It's so good to see you Helen after all these years. You mustn't leave it so long next time." While Joan poured the tea, I asked with forced cheerfulness, "Why don't you come to L.A. and stay with me for a few weeks? You could relax in the sunshine and have a break from all this weather." On queue, a percussion of rain played a brisk tattoo on the window pane and we both laughed. "Ah! Helen, that's a nice idea but Stephen couldn't travel that far and I've never been away from him for more than a day....I couldn't." she said, her voice trailing off. I searched her forty six year old face for signs of self pity or sacrifice, a tinge of bitterness maybe but saw none. Just the opposite. There was a happy lightness about her, a peaceful acceptance of things as they were. I wondered if that kind of contentment came from a nurturing kind of love but still I persisted, a need growing in me to somehow make her life better. "The way you care for Stephen is wonderful, Joan, I so admire your dedication to him and all on your own, for years now...but don't you deserve a break, a holiday, something for yourself? After all, what thanks do you ever get for all your hard work?"

The silence that filled the next moment caused my stomach to tighten. "Sorry, I shouldn't have said that." I said, lowering my eyes. Joan just leaned into me and gave me a heartfelt smile. "It's ok, Helen, she said softly, I understand what you're saying and it's a very kind thought but I'm happy here, really, I am,I have what I call, my golden moments." As she spoke she placed her teacup carefully on her saucer and turned a soft, loving face towards her son. "Those days when he smiles and I know he's not in pain, that's all the thanks I need...... my golden moments." That afternoon, in Joan's country kitchen, I learned a simple, yet universal truth that has stayed with me forever; 'that the happiness we feel in our lives is in direct proportion to the love we are able to give.'

Contributors:

 Nora Fleming joined Wicklow Writers in 2009. In her school days she loved the sound of words achieving many school awards for her short stories and poems. She has written many tributes for her family and Grandchildren marking special events. Her short stories and poems have been published in a book by Wicklow Active Retirement, "Tales of Old," and she got 3rd prize in their all-Ireland prose competition. Her writing and poetry are also published in Wicklow Writers Anthology, "Anniversary," and the Douglas Post Magazine. Nora is also a member of the 'Get Vocal' County choir and 'Avondale Voices.

Peter Hickey comes from a background in the performing arts, having previously been a professional 'cellist. He moved to Wicklow in 1995 where as well as putting pen to paper, he is now studying Yoga.

Ruth Moore has enjoyed writing poetry since secondary school. Ruth pays tribute to her secondary school English teachers, Mr Joe O' Kelly and Ms Grainne Wilson for their support and colourful way of teaching during her time at DCW. They both influenced her love of plays, poetry and prose. Because of this, Ruth's favourite writers stem from the school curriculum and include Yeats, Kavanagh and Shakespeare.

Ruth has always written in her spare time and has more recently noticed that her poetic flare has been at its finest during times of distress and heart ache! In order to veer away from this theme of melancholy, Ruth recently joined Wicklow Writers where the topics and techniques have been more ad-hoc, spontaneous and up-beat.

Academically, Ruth has a Diploma in Journalism from The Irish Academy of Public Relations and has recently started writing reviews on Scientific Lectures for the Irish Dental Nurses Magazine.

Carolann Murphy recently joined Wicklow Writers. She completed a four year degree in Psychology and Sociology at Trinity College Dublin and has a diploma in speech and drama from the London College of

Music and Dramatic Art. She is hoping to develop some writing skills, in particular to work with groups devising their own dramas or adapting existing work to suit their needs and abilities. She worked with Artistic Director Irma Gruthuis at Wicklow Youth Theatre and started Wicklow Samba and percussion project in the late 90's.

 **Helene Petersen** is Looking for her own voice in life and writing

Ganesh Ramachandran has been a member of Wicklow Writers since 2007. His creative writing work is mainly in screenplay for TV and film. He had reached the final of a few TV writers' competitions and had opportunities to shadow write for RTE's Fair City. Ganesh is a lecturer at IADT, Dun Laoghaire, in the National Film School, which also feeds his interest in TV and film production. He writes the odd bit of poetry and prose as well, and reads out loud to humans from time to time.

Edward J. Ryan joined the Wicklow Writers in 2003. Until that time his experience in writing was limited to a couple of items in a school magazine, 'Pegasus'. After joining Wicklow Writers he collaborated in the writing of two novellas, 'The Blue Rose', (unpublished), 'The Marlton Mystery', (published), two anthologies, 'Voyages' and 'Anniversary', (both published), and the production of a CD 'Voices From The Shore'. He is comfortable with most forms of writing but prefers poetry that rhymes, or at least has a distinct rhythm, and the short story genre.

Martin Swords is a member of Wicklow Writers Group. He runs Glendalough Guided Walks, giving Walks 'n Talks in the Monastic City and The Valley of Glendalough He has a background in Communications, Radio and Graphic Design. He has been writing Poetry and short stories since 1990. Martin is published in "Lifelines New and Collected", "Prairie Schooner magazine, University of Nebraska ", "Voyages" Wicklow Writers Anthology, "A View from Tiglin" "The Space Inside" Wicklow Arts Magazine, "Anniversary" Wicklow Writers Anthology;and various editions of Glendalough and Laragh News. You can also hear him read three of his poems on 'Voices from the Shore', a CD of poems and stories by Wicklow Writers. Martin has performed at many venues over the years, including Tinahely Arts Courthouse Café, Kilruddery House, Wicklow Library, The Brockagh Gallery Glendalough, the Space Inside Arts Club Wicklow and at The Fireside Sessions by the Glendalough Arts Network. He lives in Tiglin, Co. Wicklow

J. Ted Voigt is a poet and professional volunteer. He lives in Wicklow Town with his wife and two kids. He wishes he were a more diligent blogger. His latest book of poetry and short stories, Spies, Secretly, is available as a kindle ebook. The J is for Joseph, but nobody calls him that.

Belinda Walsh is a freelance Journalist and Artist. She has worked for Ashville Media and the People Newspaper Group where her stories and interviews were published in numerous national and local magazines and newspapers. She is part of the Kilmantin Gallery of Artists. Writing and Painting are her passions in life.

Vera Cait Walsh is a member of the Wicklow Writers Group where love for Creative Writing and Poetry is fostered. Her forte is Playwriting and she has been successful in having Plays performed in Galway, Cork and at the Mermaid Theatre in Bray. She also enjoys writing short stories. Part of a Creative Writing Circle with SOL Group where she facilitates Creative Writing. Organises Creative Writing Retreats in Donegal and west Cork.

Eithne Wright is a founder member of Wicklow Writers. She studied Arts as a mature student in University College, Dublin and majored in History concentrating on American Women's History and the Feminist Movement in the U.S. She admits to being a romanticist at heart and many of her short stories deal with romantic situations and how they are resolved. Some of her poems are published in Siochan, the magazine for retired members of An Garda Siochana.

Made in the USA
Charleston, SC
28 August 2014